The Jewish Kids' Hebrew–English Wordbook

by Chaya M. Burstein

THE JEWISH PUBLICATION SOCIETY
Philadelphia and Jerusalem
5754/1993

*This book is dedicated
to Naomi Meira,
who is just starting out.*

דֶּרֶךְ צְלֵחָה!

Dedicated in loving memory of
ESTHER HOFFMAN BELLER
(1893-1991),
a teacher who loved books,
by her cousin, David Wolfson;
her second cousins,
Dr. Philip Wolfson, Mrs. Toby Risman,
Robert Wolfson; and her third cousins,
Eric Wolfson, Shoshana Risman, Daniella Risman.

Copyright © 1993 by Chaya M. Burstein
First edition. All rights reserved.
Manufactured in the United States of America.
Book design by Emily Sper

Library of Congress Cataloging in Publication Data

Burstein, Chaya M.
    The Jewish kids' Hebrew-English wordbook/by Chaya M. Burstein.
    p. cm.
    Includes index.
    Summary: Presents pictures for 500 Hebrew words, with the
English equivalent, grouped by subjects such as family, holidays,
animals, work, and play.
    ISBN 0—8276—0381—9
    1. Hebrew language — Dictionaries. Juvenile — English.
2. Picture dictionaries, Hebrew. [1. Hebrew language —
Dictionaries. 2. Picture dictionaries, Hebrew.] I. Title.
PJ4833.B87 1993   92—3971
492.4'321 — dc20   *25203446*   CIP
                                                        AC

10 9 8 7 6 5 4 3 2 1

HI! I'm Kofee. Look for me
on each page. If you can't read
Hebrew yet, read the syllables
under the Hebrew word. Stress
the letters in **bold** type and
follow this guide:

ai as in say
a or **ah** as in arm
e or **eh** as in bed
ei as in bite
i as in hit
ee as in tree
o as in no
oo as in noon
h as in hat
ḥ as in ḥallah or bleḥ
s as in see
sh as in shin

CONTENTS

Your Family and Your Home 4–5
You and Your Room 6–7
Here's how to say . . . 8–9
The Neighborhood 10–11
Synagogue/Temple 12
Ritual Objects 13
School and Playground 14–15
Holiday Greetings 16
Holidays 16–20
The Week 21
Seasons 22
Numbers 23
Happy Times 24–25
Sad Times 26
Good Deeds 27
The State of Israel 28–29
In the Country 30–31
In the Kitchen 32–33
Animals 34–35
Work and Play 36
Dictionary 37–39

Your Family and Your Home הַמִּשְׁפָּחָה שֶׁלְּךָ וְהַבַּיִת שֶׁלְּךָ

house
בַּיִת
ba-yeet

bathtub
אַמְבַּטְיָה
am-**bat**-yah

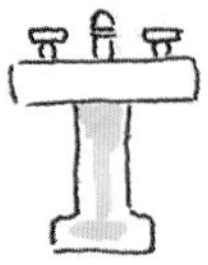

sink
כִּיּוֹר
kee-**yor**

toilet
אַסְלָה
as-**lah**

cat
חָתוּל
ḥa-**tool**

dog
כֶּלֶב
ke-lev

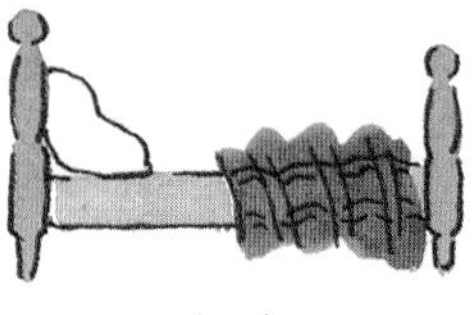

bed
מִטָּה
mee-**tah**

table
שֻׁלְחָן
shool-**ḥan**

broom
מַטְאֲטֵא
mat-a-**tai**

stairs
מַדְרֵגוֹת
mad-rai-**got**

television
טֶלֶוִיזְיָה
te-le-**veez**-yah

ha-mish-pa-**ḥah** shel-**ḥah** vi-ha-**ba**-yeet shel-**ḥah**

computer
מַחְשֵׁב
maḥ-**shaiv**

family
מִשְׁפָּחָה
mish-pa-**ḥah**

baby
תִּינוֹק
tee-**nok**

fireplace
אָח
aḥ

grandfather
סַבָּא
sa-bah

grandmother
סַבְתָּא
sav-tah

sister
אָחוֹת
a-**ḥot**

aunt
דוֹדָה
do-**dah**

uncle
דוֹד
dod

cousin
בֶּן–דוֹד
ben-**dod**

mother
אִמָּא
ee-mah

father
אַבָּא
a-bah

brother
אָח
aḥ

You and Your Room אַתָּה וְהַחֶדֶר שֶׁלְּךָ a-**tah** vi-ha-**ḥe**-der shel-**ḥah**

clock
שָׁעוֹן
sha-**on**

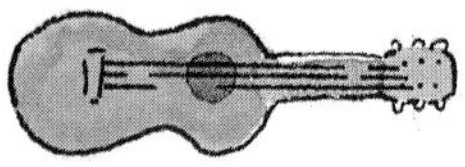

guitar
גִּיטָרָה
gee-**ta**-rah

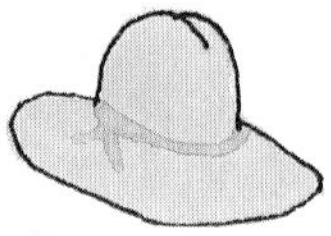

hat
כּוֹבַע
ko-vah

boots
מַגָּפַיִם
ma-ga-**fa**-yeem

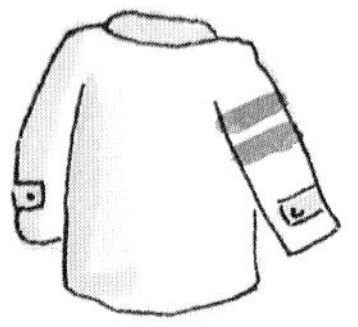

jacket
מְעִיל
mi-**eel**

dress
שִׂמְלָה
sim-**lah**

skirt
חֲצָאִית
ḥa-tza-**eet**

shirt
חֻלְצָה
ḥool-**tzah**

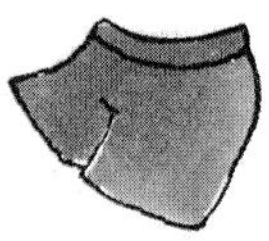

shorts
מִכְנָסַיִם קְצָרִים
miḥ-na-**sa**-yeem ki-tza-**reem**

pajamas
פִּיגָ'מָה
pee-**ja**-mah

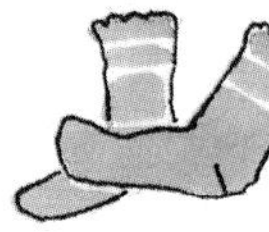

socks
גַּרְבַּיִם
gar-**ba**-yeem

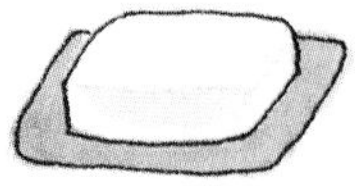

soap
סַבּוֹן
sa-**bon**

radio
רַדְיוֹ
ra-dee-o

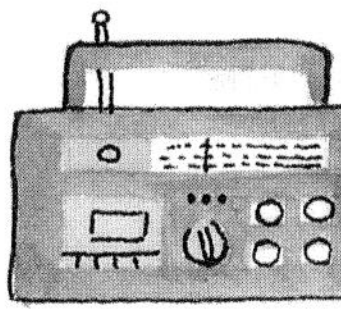

calendar
לוּחַ שָׁנָה
loo-aḥ sha-**na**

shower
מִקְלַחַת
mik-**la**-ḥat

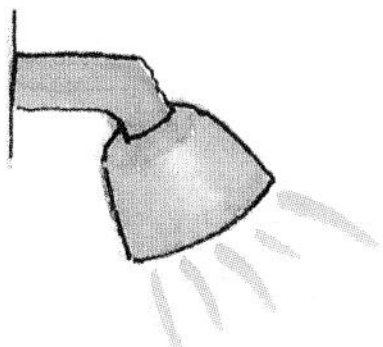

window
חַלּוֹן
ḥa-**lon**

daughter
בַּת
bat

braids
צַמּוֹת
tza-**mot**

son
בֵּן
ben

stool
סַפְסָל
saf-**sal**

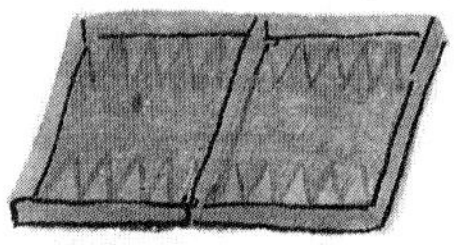

game
מִשְׂחָק
mis-**ḥak**

toothbrush
מִבְרֶשֶׁת שִׁנַּיִם
miv-**re**-shet shee-**na**-yeem

knee
בֶּרֶךְ
be-reḥ

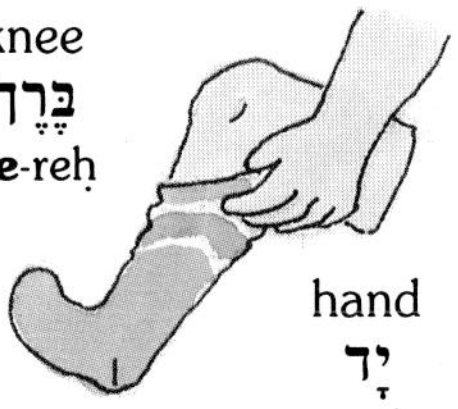

foot
רֶגֶל
re-gel

hand
יָד
yad

nose
אַף
af

eye
עַיִן
a-yin

hair
שֵׂעָר
sai-**ar**

mouth
פֶּה
peh

ear
אֹזֶן
o-zen

teeth
שִׁנַּיִם
shee-**na**-yeem

head
רֹאשׁ
rosh

Here's how to say . . .

כָּכָה אוֹמְרִים **ka**-ḥa om-**reem**

I love you.
אֲנִי אוֹהֶבֶת אוֹתךְ
a-**nee** o-**he**-vet ot-**ḥah**
Happy birthday.
יוֹם הֻלֶּדֶת שָׂמֵחַ
yom hoo-**le**-det sa-**mai**-aḥ
Wow, super!
שִׂגָּעוֹן
shee-ga-**on**
Hearty appetite.
בְּתֵאָבוֹן
bi-**tai**-a-**von**
Thanks.
תּוֹדָה
to-**dah**
No.
לֹא
lo
Yes.
כֵּן
ken
Please.
בְּבַקָּשָׁה
bi-va-ka-**sha**
Oh, no!
אוֹי וַאֲבוֹי
oy va-a-**voy**
DAILY BLAB
How do you say . . . ?
אֵיךְ אוֹמְרִים
aiḥ om-**reem**
Wear it well.
תִּתְחַדְּשִׁי
tit-ḥad-**shee**
Good night.
לַיְלָה טוֹב
lei-lah tov
Sweet dreams.
חֲלוֹמוֹת פָּז
ḥa-lo-**mot** paz

The Neighborhood הַשְׁכוּנָה ha-sh-ḥoo-**nah**

store
חָנוּת
ḥa-**noot**

grocery store
מַכֹּלֶת
ma-**ko**-let

dancing school
בֵּית סֵפֶר לְרִקּוּד
bait **se**-fer li-ree-**kood**

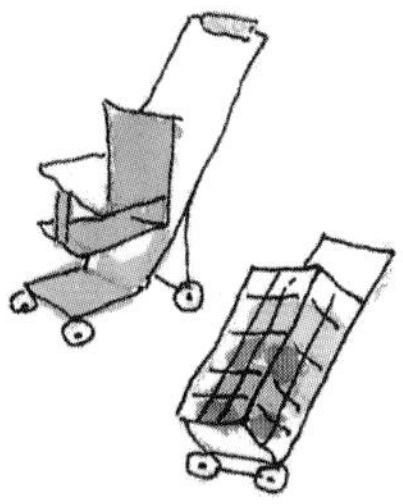

stroller, shopping cart
עֲגָלָה
a-ga-**lah**

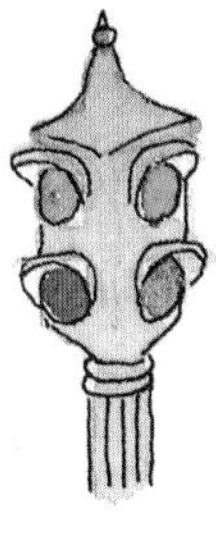

traffic light
רַמְזוֹר
ram-**zor**

mailman
דַּוָּר
da-**var**

apartment
דִּירָה
dee-**rah**

toys
צַעֲצוּעִים
tza-a-tzoo-**eem**

Jeep
גִ׳יפּ
jeep

truck
מַשָּׂאִית
ma-sa-**eet**

bus
אוֹטוֹבּוּס
o-to-boos

movie house
קוֹלְנוֹעַ
kol-**no**-ah

bicycle
אוֹפַנַּיִם
o-fa-**na**-yeem

motorcycle
אוֹפַנּוֹעַ
o-fa-**no**-ah

policewoman
שׁוֹטֶרֶת
sho-**te**-ret

post office
דֹּאַר
do-ar

car
מְכוֹנִית
mi-ḥo-**neet**

basketball
כַּדּוּר סַל
ka-**door sal**

Synagogue/Temple בֵּית הַכְּנֶסֶת bait ha-**kne**-set

rabbi
רַב
rav

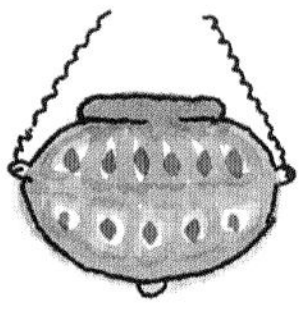

eternal light
נֵר תָּמִיד
ner ta-**meed**

ark
אָרוֹן
a-**ron**

ark curtain
פָּרֹכֶת
pa-**ro**-ḥet

prayer shawl
טַלִּית
ta-**leet**

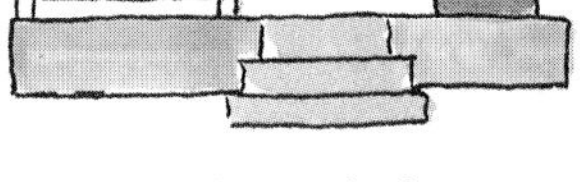

reading platform
בִּמָה
bee-**mah**

prayer book
סִדּוּר
see-**door**

cantor
חַזָּן
ḥa-**zan**

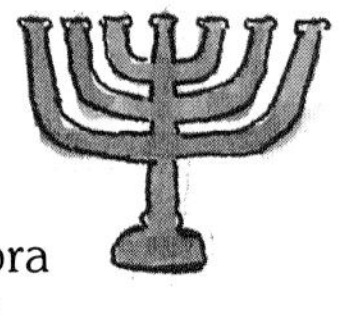

candelabra
מְנוֹרָה
mi-no-**rah**

Ritual Objects כְּלֵי קוֹדֶשׁ klai **ko**-desh

phylacteries (tefillin)
תְּפִלִּין
ti-fee-**leen**

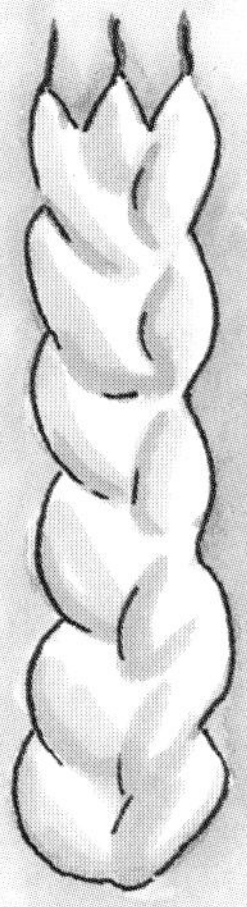

havdalah candle
נֵר הַבְדָּלָה
ner hav-da-**lah**

crown
כֶּתֶר
ke-ter

Torah
תּוֹרָה
to-**rah**

breastplate
חֹשֶׁן
ḥo-shen

Torah mantle
מְעִיל הַתּוֹרָה
mi-**eel** ha-to-**rah**

bells
פַּעֲמוֹנִים
pa-a-mo-**neem**

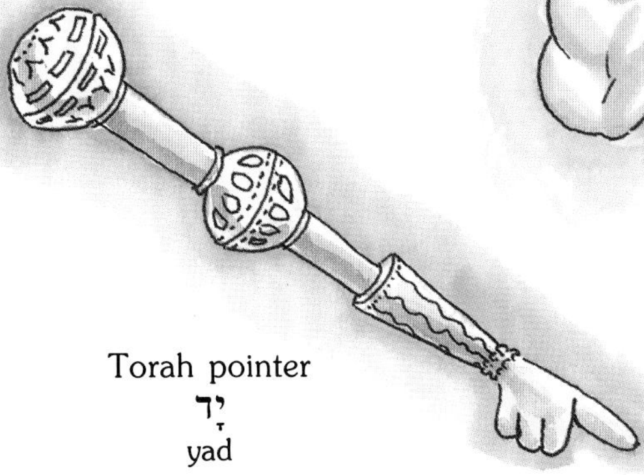

Torah pointer
יָד
yad

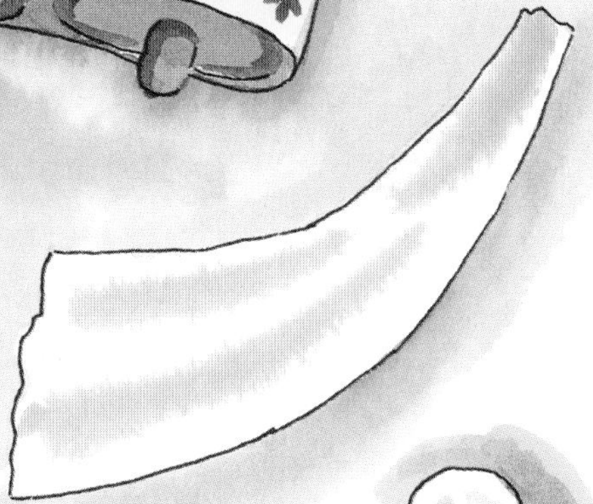

ram's horn
שׁוֹפָר
sho-**far**

spice box
קוּפְסַת בְּשָׂמִים
koof-**sat** bi-sa-**meem**

Purim scroll
מְגִלָּה
mi-gee-**lah**

mezuzah
מְזוּזָה
mi-zoo-**zah**

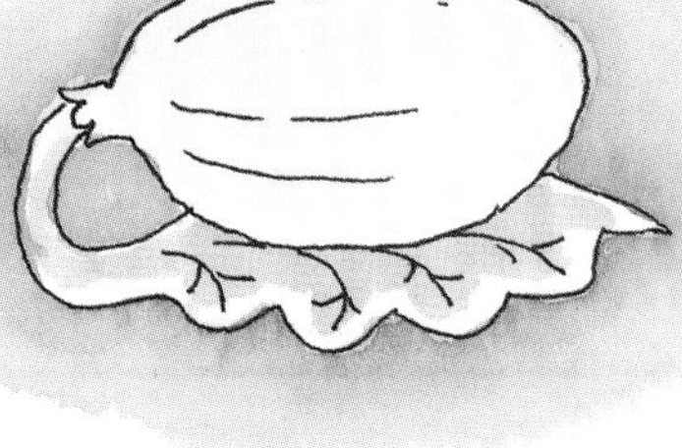

etrog box
קוּפְסַת אֶתְרוֹג
koof-**sat** et-**rog**

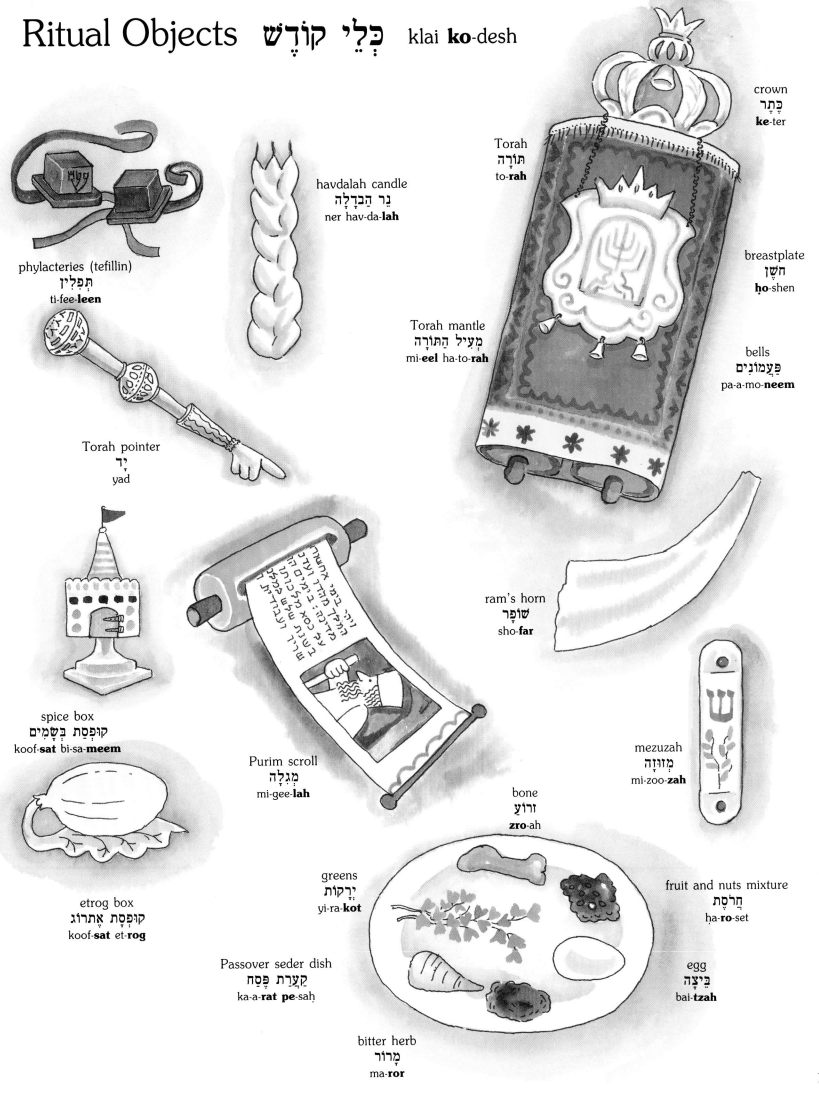

bone
זְרוֹעַ
zro-ah

greens
יְרָקוֹת
yi-ra-**kot**

fruit and nuts mixture
חֲרֹסֶת
ḥa-**ro**-set

Passover seder dish
קַעֲרַת פֶּסַח
ka-a-**rat** **pe**-saḥ

egg
בֵּיצָה
bai-**tzah**

bitter herb
מָרוֹר
ma-**ror**

School and Playground בֵּית סֵפֶר וְגַן מִשְׂחָקִים bait **se**-fer

map
מַפָּה
ma-**pah**

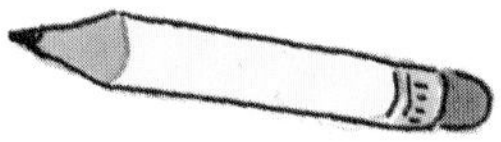

pencil
עִפָּרוֹן
ee-pa-**ron**

bulletin board
לוּחַ
loo-aḥ

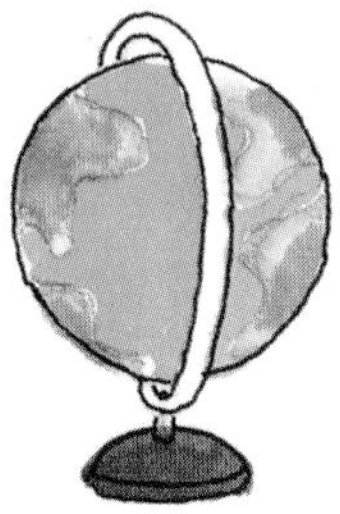

globe
גלוֹבּוּס
glo-boos

eyeglasses
מִשְׁקָפַיִם
mish-ka-**fa**-yeem

earrings
עֲגִילִים
a-gee-**leem**

books
סְפָרִים
s'fa-**reem**

teacher
מוֹרָה
mo-**rah**

student
תַּלְמִיד
tal-**meed**

bookbag
תִּיק
teek

oo-**gan** mis-ḥa-**keem**

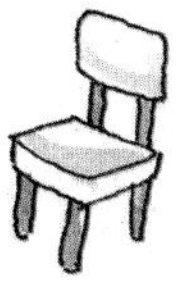

chair
כִּסֵּא
kee-**sai**

slide
מַגְלֵשָׁה
mag-lai-**shah**

swing
or see-saw
נַדְנֵדָה
nad-nai-**dah**

climbing bars
סוּלָּמֶת
soo-**le**-met

principal
מְנַהֶלֶת
mi-na-**he**-let

notebook
מַחְבֶּרֶת
maḥ-**be**-ret

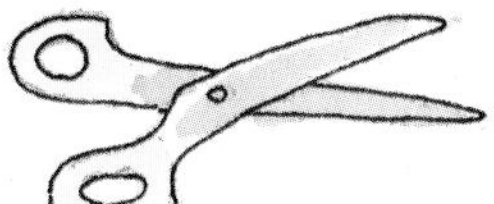

scissors
מִסְפָּרַיִם
mis-pa-**ra**-yeem

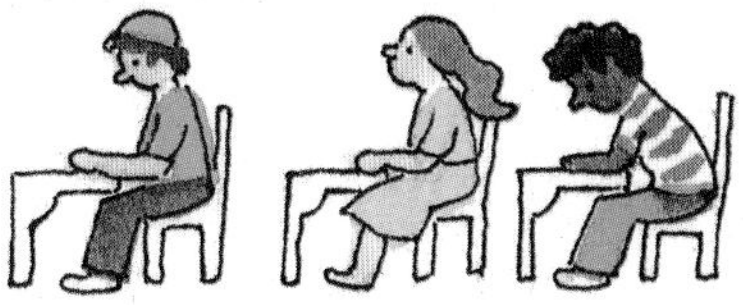

class
כִּתָּה
kee-**tah**

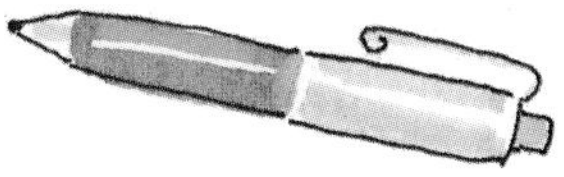

pen
עֵט
et

Holiday Greetings

אִחוּלִים לַחַג ee-ḥoo-**leem** la-**ḥag**

Peaceful and blessed Sabbath.
שַׁבַּת שָׁלוֹם וּמְבֹרָךְ
sha-**bat** sha-**lom** oo-mi-vo-**raḥ**

Happy holiday.
חַג שָׂמֵחַ
ḥag sa-**mai**-aḥ

Good week.
שָׁבוּעַ טוֹב
sha-**voo**-a tov

Happy Hanukkah
חֲנֻכָּה שָׂמֵחַ
ḥa-noo-kah sa-**mai**-aḥ

May you be
written down for a good year.
לְשָׁנָה טוֹבָה תִּכָּתֵבוּ
li-sha-**nah** to-**vah** tee-ka-**tai**-voo

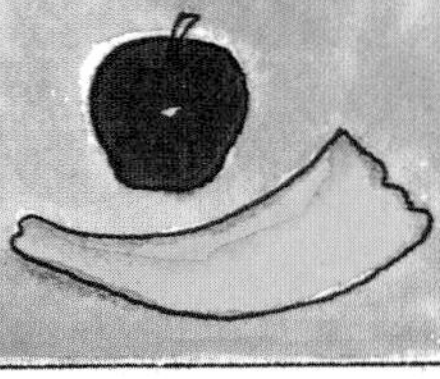

May you be written and sealed
for a good year.
לְשָׁנָה טוֹבָה תִּכָּתֵבוּ וְתֵחָתֵמוּ
li-sha-**nah** to-**vah** tee-ka-**tai**-voo vi-tai-ḥa-**tai**-moo

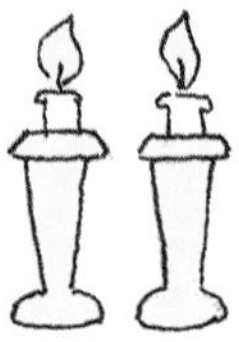

candles
נֵרוֹת
nai-**rot**

Sabbath bread, hallah
חַלָּה
ḥa-**lah**

wine
יַיִן
ya-yeen

Holidays חַגִּים ḥa-**geem**

New Year's cards
כַּרְטִיסֵי בְּרָכָה
kar-tee-**sai** bi-ra-**ḥa**

prayer book for High Holidays
מַחְזוֹר
maḥ-**zor**

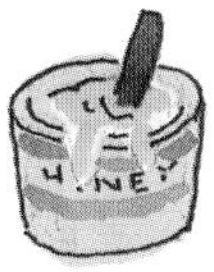

honey
דְּבַשׁ
d'vash

star
כּוֹכָב
ko-**ḥav**

squirrel
סְנָאִי
sna-**ee**

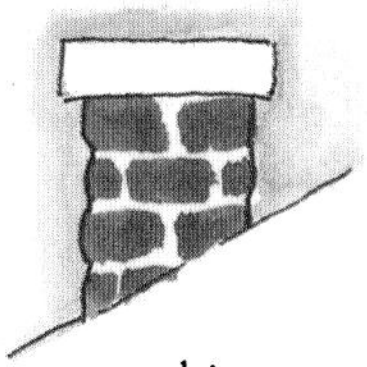

chimney
אֲרֻבָּה
a-roo-**bah**

booth (sukkah)
סוּכָּה
soo-**kah**

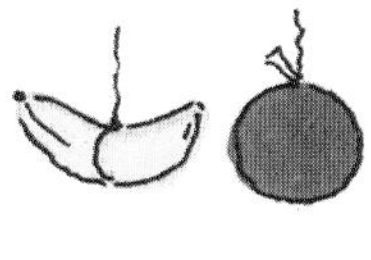

fruit
פֵּרוֹת
pai-**rot**

guests
אוֹרְחִים
or-**ḥeem**

citron
אֶתְרוֹג
et-**rog**

lulav
(branches of willow, myrtle, and palm)
לוּלָב
loo-**lav**

Holidays חַגִּים ḥa-**geem**

Torah parade
הַקָּפוֹת
ha-ka-**fot**

flag
דֶּגֶל
de-gel

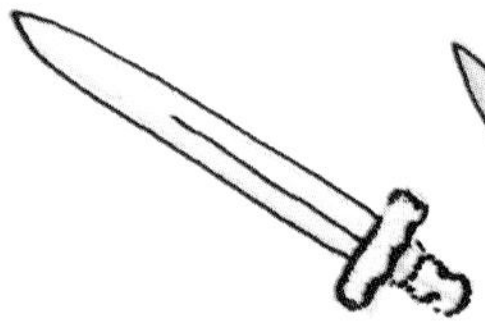

sword
חֶרֶב
ḥe-rev

elephant
פִּיל
peel

soldier
חַיָּל
ḥa-**yal**

Simhat Torah
שִׂמְחַת תּוֹרָה
sim-**ḥat** to-**rah**

Hanukkah
חֲנֻכָּה
ḥa-noo-kah

Maccabees
מַכַּבִּים
ma-ka-**beem**

top (dreidel)
סְבִיבוֹן
si-vee-**von**

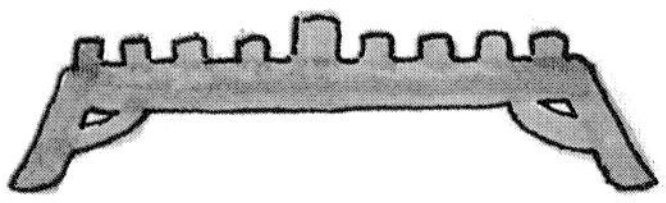

Hanukkah lamp
חֲנֻכִּיָּה
ḥa-noo-kee-**yah**

seder book
(haggadah)
הַגָּדָה
ha-ga-**dah**

Tu Bi-Sh'vat
ט״ו בִּשְׁבָט
too bi-**shvat**

Purim
פּוּרִים
poo-**reem**

Passover
פֶּסַח
pe-saḥ

boy
יֶלֶד
ye-led

girl
יַלְדָה
yal-**dah**

tree
עֵץ
etz

goat
עֵז
ez

noisemaker
רַעֲשָׁן
ra-a-**shan**

king
מֶלֶךְ
me-leḥ

queen
מַלְכָּה
mal-**kah**

PURIM PEOPLE

Passover seder
סֵדֶר פֶּסַח
se-der **pe**-saḥ

Ahashveros
אֲחַשְׁוֵרוֹשׁ
a-ḥash-**vai**-rosh

Mordecai
מָרְדְּכַי
mor-di-**ḥei**

Haman
הָמָן
ha-**man**

Esther
אֶסְתֵּר
es-**ter**

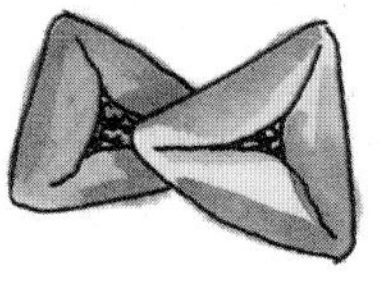

Purim pastries
אָזְנֵי הָמָן
oz-**nai** ha-**man**

Holidays חַגִים ha-**geem**

campfire
מְדוּרָה
mi-doo-**rah**

children
יְלָדִים
yi-la-**deem**

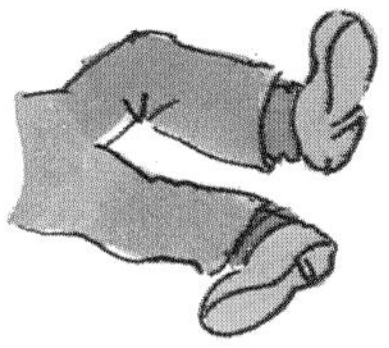

shoes
נַעֲלַיִם
na-a-**la**-yeem

night
לַיְלָה
lei-lah

parade
מִצְעָד
mee-**tzad**

Lag Ba'Omer
לַ"ג בָּעֹמֶר
lag ba-**o**-mer

Israel Independence Day
יוֹם הָעַצְמָאוּת
yom ha-atz-ma-**oot**

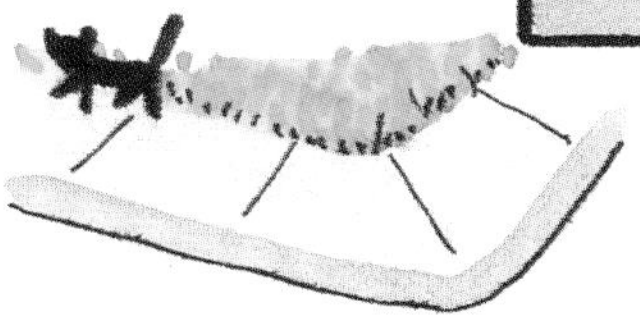

sidewalk
מִדְרָכָה
mid-ra-**ḥah**

sun
שֶׁמֶשׁ
she-mesh

clouds
עֲנָנִים
a-na-**neem**

Moses
מֹשֶׁה
mo-**sheh**

Mount Sinai
הַר סִינַי
har see-**nei**

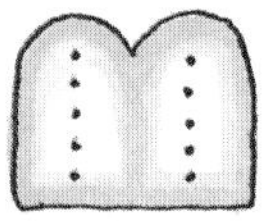

Ten Commandments
עֲשֶׂרֶת הַדִּבְּרוֹת
a-**se**-ret ha-dee-**brot**

People of Israel
עַם יִשְׂרָאֵל
am yis-ra-**el**

The Week

הַשָּׁבוּעַ ha-sha-**voo**-ah

Sunday
יוֹם רִאשׁוֹן
yom ree-**shon**

Monday
יוֹם שֵׁנִי
yom shai-**nee**

Tuesday
יוֹם שְׁלִישִׁי
yom shlee-**shee**

Wednesday
יוֹם רְבִיעִי
yom ri-vee-**ee**

Thursday
יוֹם חֲמִישִׁי
yom ḥa-mee-**shee**

Friday
יוֹם שִׁשִּׁי
yom shee-**shee**

Saturday
שַׁבָּת
sha-**bat**

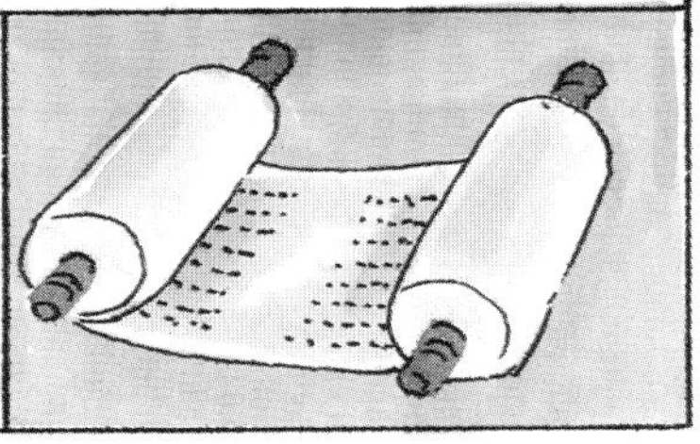

Seasons עוֹנוֹת o-**not**

autumn
סְתָו
s'tav

Autumn holidays: Rosh Hashanah
Yom Kippur
Sukkot
Simhat Torah

Winter holidays: Ḥanukkah
Tu Bi-Sh'vat
Purim

winter
חֹרֶף
ḥo-ref

spring
אָבִיב
a-**veev**

Spring holidays: Passover
Holocaust Remembrance Day
Israel Independence Day
Lag Ba'Omer

Summer holidays: Shavuot
Tisha B'Av

summer
קַיִץ
ka-yeetz

Numbers מִסְפָּרִים mis-pa-**reem**

one
אֶחָד
e-**ḥad**

1

God
אֱלֹהִים
e-lo-**heem**

two
שְׁנַיִם
shna-yeem

2

Adam and Eve

three
שְׁלֹשָׁה
shlo-**shah**

3

The Patriarchs

Abraham
Isaac
Jacob

4

four
אַרְבָּעָה
ar-ba-**ah**

Sarah
Rivka
Leah
Raḥel

The Matriarchs

Vashti   Esther
Mordecai   Haman   Ahashveros

5

Purim People

five
חֲמִשָּׁה
ḥa-mee-**shah**

six
שִׁשָּׁה
shee-**shah**

6

Ḥanukkah Heroes
Mattathias
Simon
Jonathan
Judah
Eliezer
Johanan

seven
שִׁבְעָה
sheev-**ah**

7

7 Days in a Week

1 2 3 4 5 6 7

eight
שְׁמוֹנָה
shmo-**nah**

8

8 Ḥanukkah candles
plus the Shamash

9

nine
תִּשְׁעָה
teesh-**ah**

Noah and 8 Passengers

10 Commandments

10

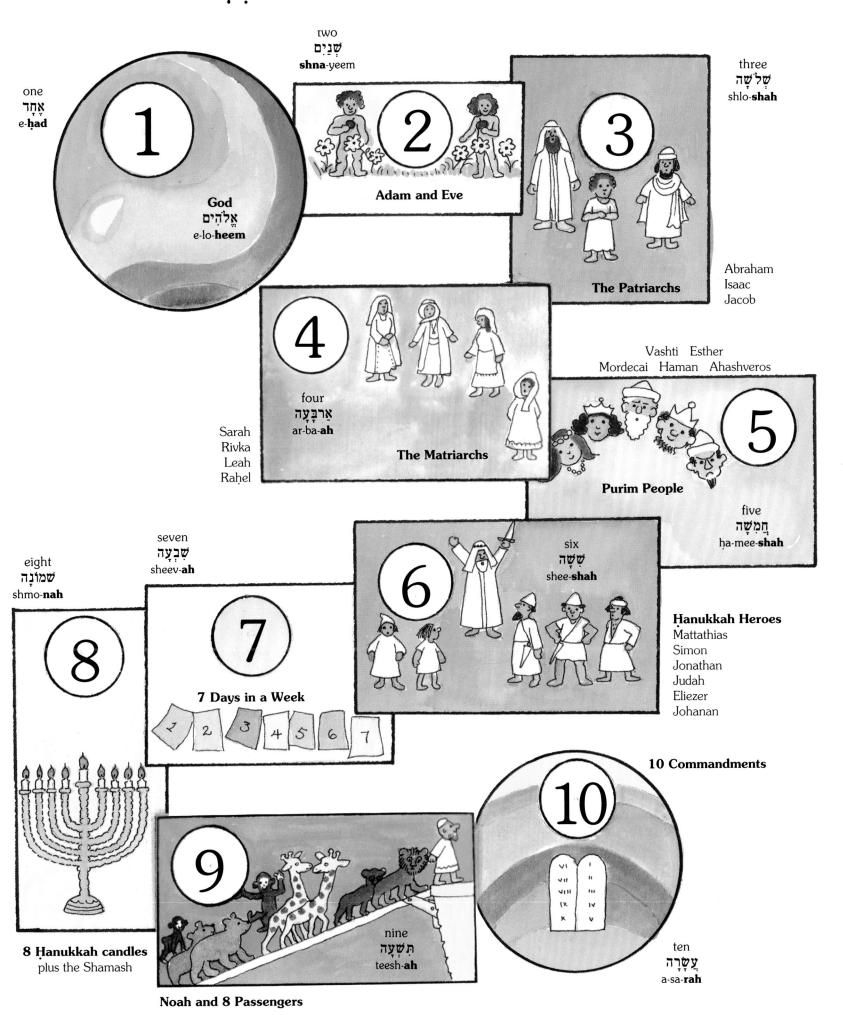

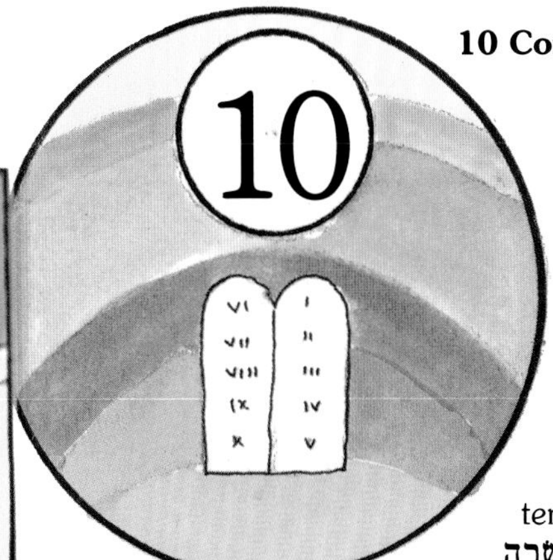

ten
עֲשָׂרָה
a-sa-**rah**

Happy Times שְׂמָחוֹת se-ma-**ḥot**

bridal canopy
חֻפָּה
ḥoo-**pah**

bride
כַּלָּה
ka-**lah**

groom
חָתָן
ḥa-**tan**

in-laws
מְחֻתָּנִים
mi-ḥoo-ta-**neem**

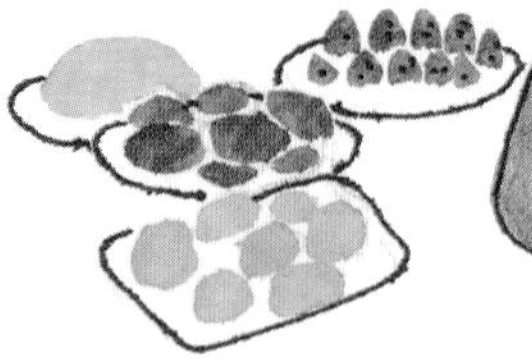

food
אֹכֶל
o-ḥel

wedding
חֲתוּנָה
ḥa-too-**nah**

birthday
יוֹם הֻלֶּדֶת
yom hoo-**le**-det

violin
כִּנּוֹר
kee-**nor**

clarinet
קְלַרְנִית
klar-**neet**

musicians
מוּזִיקָאִים
mu-zee-ka-**eem**

friends
חֲבֵרִים
ḥa-ve-**reem**

naming ceremony
שִׂמְחַת הַבַּת
seem-ḥat ha-bat

confirmation
הַכְנָסָה בִּבְרִית הַדָּת
haḥ-na-sah bi-vreet ha-dat

bar/bat mitzvah
בַּר/בַּת מִצְוָה
bar/bat mitz-vah

circumciser (mohel)
מוֹהֵל
mo-hel

godfather
סַנְדָּק
san-dak

Elijah's chair
כִּסֵּא אֵלִיָּהוּ
kee-sai e-lee-ya-hoo

baby girl
תִּנוֹקֶת
tee-no-ket

baby boy
תִּינוֹק
tee-nok

a reading from Prophets
הַפְטָרָה
haf-ta-rah

birthday cake
עֻגַת יוֹם הֻלֶּדֶת
oo-gat yom hoo-le-det

flowers
פְּרָחִים
pra-heem

guests
אוֹרְחִים
or-ḥeem

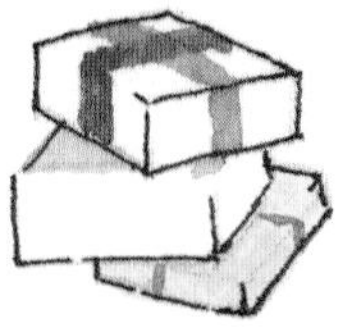

gifts
מַתָּנוֹת
ma-ta-not

Sad Times יְמֵי עֶצֶב yi-**mai e**-tzev

Holy Temple
בֵּית הַמִּקְדָּשׁ
bait ha-mik-**dash**

memorial lamp
נֵר נְשָׁמָה
ner ni-sha-**mah**

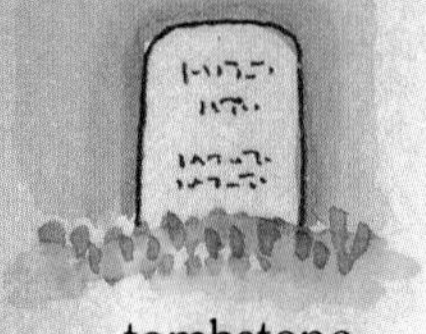

tombstone
מַצֵּבָה
ma-tzai-**vah**

cemetery
בֵּית קְבָרוֹת
bait ke-va-**rot**

mourner
אָבֵל
ah-**vail**

Ninth of Av
(Tisha B'Av)
תִּשְׁעָה בְּאָב
tee-**shah** bi-**av**

Holocaust Remembrance Day
יוֹם הַשׁוֹאָה
yom ha-sho-**ah**

funeral
הַלְוָיָה
ha-li-va-**yah**

seven days of mourning
שִׁבְעָה
sheev-**ah**

Good Deeds מַעֲשִׂים טוֹבִים ma-a-**seem** to-**veem**

Torah study
לִמּוּד תּוֹרָה
lee-**mood** to-**rah**

commandment
(good deed)
מִצְוָה
mitz-**vah**

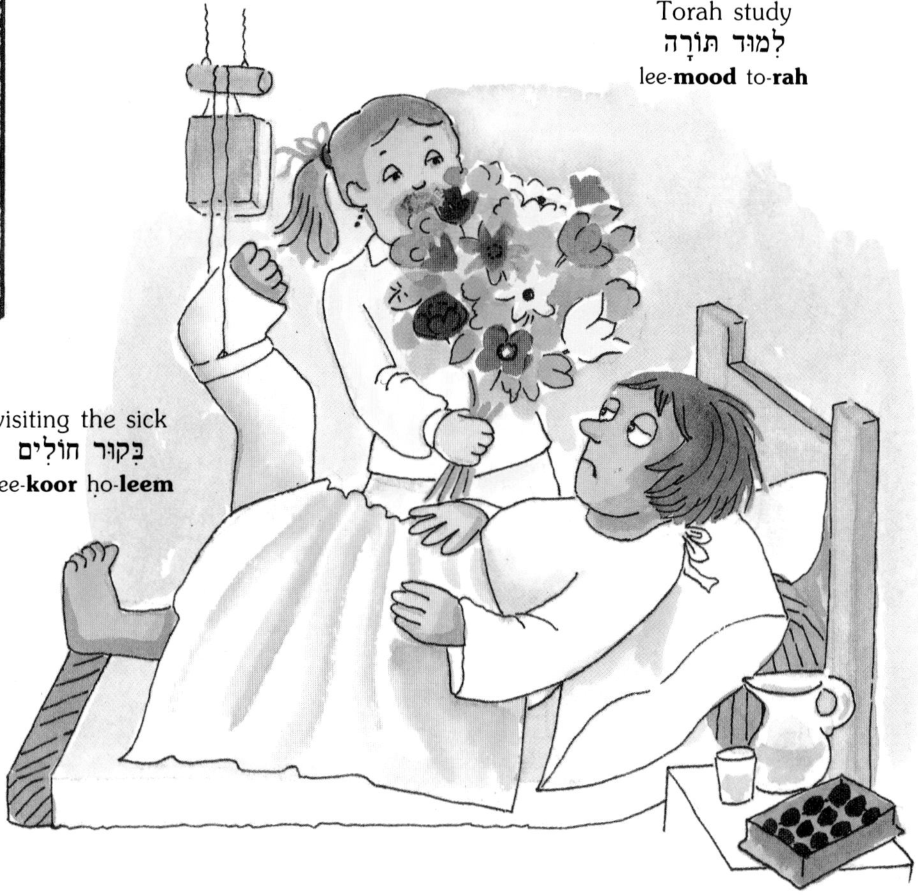

visiting the sick
בִּקּוּר חוֹלִים
bee-**koor** ḥo-**leem**

charity
צְדָקָה
tzi-da-**kan**

kindness to animals
צַעַר בַּעֲלֵי חַיִּים
tza-ar ba-a-**lai** ḥa-**yeem**

responsibility for each other
עֲרֵבוּת הֲדָדִית
a-rai-**voot** ha-da-**deet**

The State of Israel מְדִינַת יִשְׂרָאֵל mi-dee-**nat** yis-ra-**el**

tank
טַנְק
tank

village
כְּפָר
kfar

kibbutz
קִבּוּץ
kee-**bootz**

tourists
תַּיָּרִים
ta-ya-**reem**

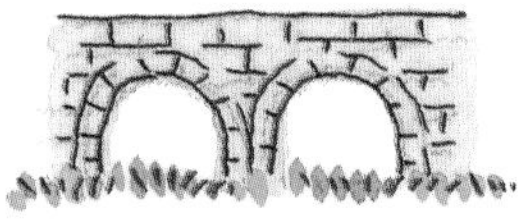

aqueduct
מוֹבִיל מַיִם
mo-**veel ma**-yeem

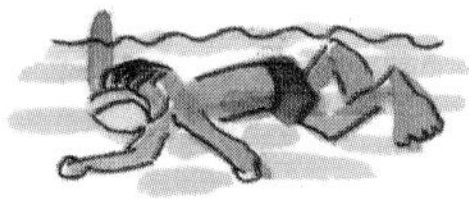

snorkel
שְׁנוֹרְקֶל
shnor-kel

mosque
מִסְגָּד
mis-**gad**

parliament of Israel
כְּנֶסֶת
kne-set

windsurfer
גַּלְשָׁן
gal-**shan**

felafel sandwich
פְּלָפֶל וּפִתָּה
fe-**la**-fel vi-**pee**-tah

factory
בֵּית חֲרֹשֶׁת
bait ḥa-**ro**-shet

city
עִיר
eer

church
כְּנֵסִיָּה
knai-see-**ah**

cactus
צַבָּר
tza-**var**

fighter plane
מְטוֹס קְרָב
mi-**tos** krav

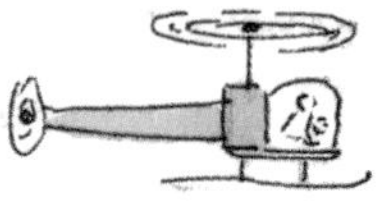

helicopter
מַסּוֹק
ma-**sok**

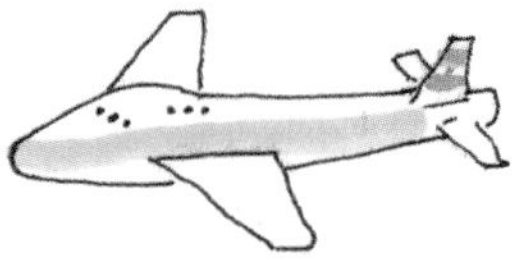

passenger plane
מְטוֹס נוֹסְעִים
mi-**tos** nos-**eem**

sea
יָם
yam

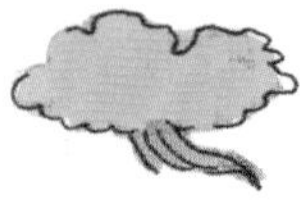

olive tree
עֵץ זַיִת
etz **za**-yeet

orange tree
עֵץ תַּפּוּזִים
etz ta-poo-**zeem**

palm tree
דֶּקֶל
de-kel

Arab
עֲרָבִי
a-ra-**vee**

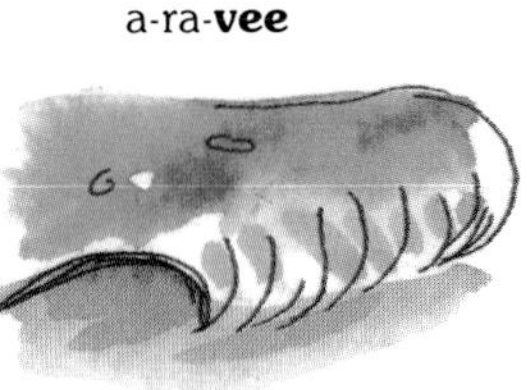

wave
גַּל
gal

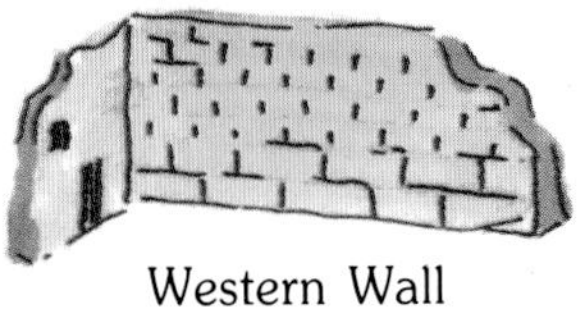

Western Wall
הַכֹּתֶל הַמַּעֲרָבִי
ha-**ko**-tel ha-ma-a-ra-**vee**

market
שׁוּק
shook

soldier
חַיָּל
ḥa-**yal**

ultra-Orthodox Jew
יְהוּדִי חֲרֵדִי
yi-hoo-**dee** ḥa-rai-**dee**

In the Country בַּכְּפָר ba-**kfar**

train
רַכֶּבֶת
ra-**ke**-vet

barn
רֶפֶת
re-fet

cow
פָּרָה
pa-**rah**

tractor
טְרַקְטוֹר
trak-tor

farmers
אִכָּרִים
ee-ka-**reem**

bridge
גֶּשֶׁר
ge-sher

river
נָהָר
na-**har**

hike
טִיּוּל
tee-**yool**

summer camp
מַחֲנֶה קַיִץ
ma-ḥa-**neh** **ka**-yitz

chicken
תַּרְנְגֹלֶת
tar-ni-**go**-let

horse
סוּס
soos

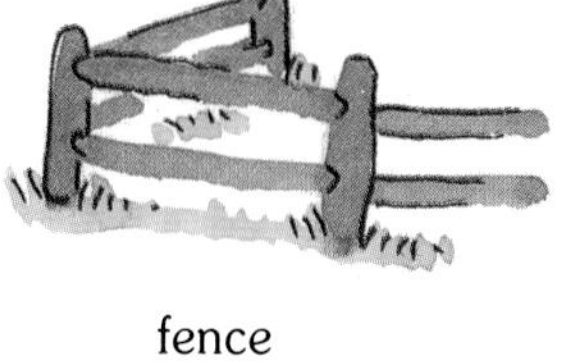

fence
גָּדֵר
ga-**der**

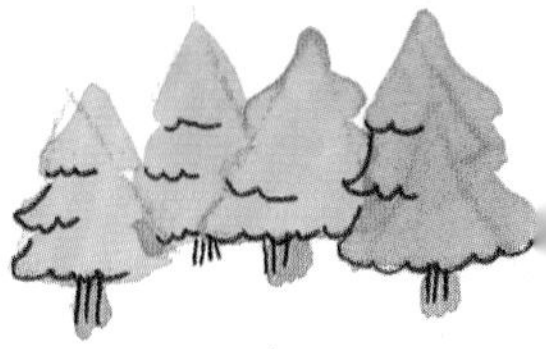

woods
יַעַר
ya-ar

tent
אֹהֶל
o-hel

skunk
בּוֹאֵשׁ
bo-**esh**

singing group
מַקְהֵלָה
ma-kai-**lah**

lake
אֲגַם
a-**gam**

bush
שִׂיחַ
see-aḥ

circle dance
(hora)
הוֹרָה
ho-rah

fish
דָּג
dag

fisherman
דַּיָּג
da-**yag**

In the Kitchen בַּמִּטְבָּח ba-mit-**baḥ**

dairy
חֲלָבִי
ḥa-la-**vee**

meat
(non-dairy & non-parve)
בְּשָׂרִי
bi-sa-**ree**

parve
פָּרְוֶה
par-ve

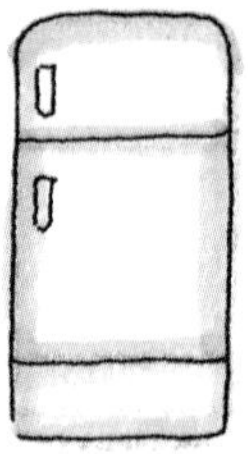

refrigerator
מְקָרֵר
mi-ka-**rer**

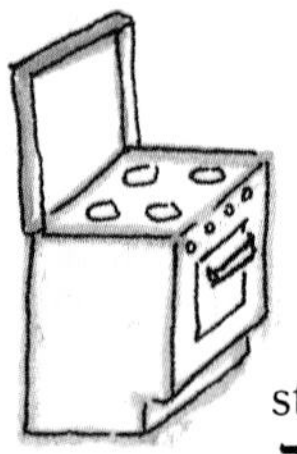

stove
תַּנּוּר
ta-**noor**

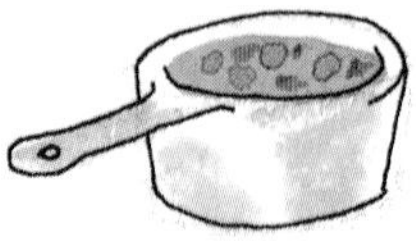

pot
סִיר
seer

soup
מָרָק
ma-**rak**

chicken
(food)
עוֹף
of

meat
בָּשָׂר
ba-**sar**

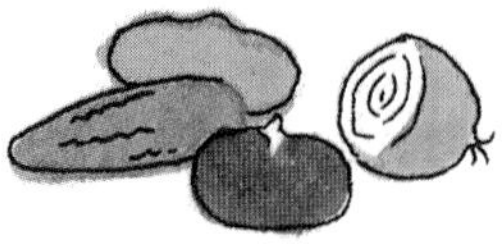

vegetables
יְרָקוֹת
yi-ra-**kot**

fruit
פֵּרוֹת
pai-**rot**

cheese
גְּבִינָה
gvee-**nah**

dish
צַלַּחַת
tza-**la**-ḥat

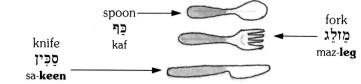

spoon
כַּף
kaf

fork
מַזְלֵג
maz-**leg**

knife
סַכִּין
sa-**keen**

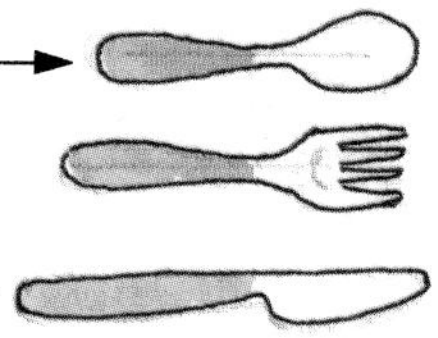

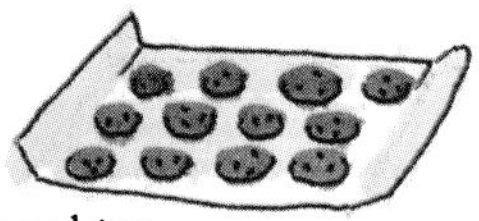

cookies
עוּגִיּוֹת
oo-gee-**ot**

flour
קֶמַח
ke-maḥ

eggs
בֵּיצִים
bai-**tzeem**

salt
מֶלַח
me-laḥ

sugar
סֻכָּר
soo-**kar**

bread
לֶחֶם
le-ḥem

jam
רִיבָּה
ree-**bah**

milk
חָלָב
ḥa-**lav**

glass
כּוֹס
kos

water
מַיִם
mah-yeem

cup
סֵפֶל
se-fel

garbage
אַשְׁפָּה
ash-**pah**

ice cream
גְלִידָה
glee-**dah**

butter
חֶמְאָה
ḥem-**ah**

Animals בַּעֲלֵי חַיִּים ba-a-**lai** ḥa-**yeem**

dinosaur
דִּינוֹסָאוּרוּס
dee-no-sa-**oo**-roos

bee
דְבוֹרָה
dvo-**rah**

butterfly
פַּרְפַּר
par-**par**

parrot
תֻּכִּי
too-kee

woodpecker
נַקָּר
na-**kar**

lion
אַרְיֵה
ar-**yai**

turtle
צָב
tzav

elephant
פִּיל
peel

wolf
זְאֵב
z'aiv

fox
שׁוּעָל
shoo-**al**

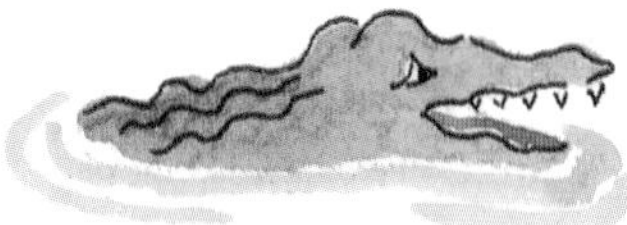

crocodile
תַּנִּין
ta-**neen**

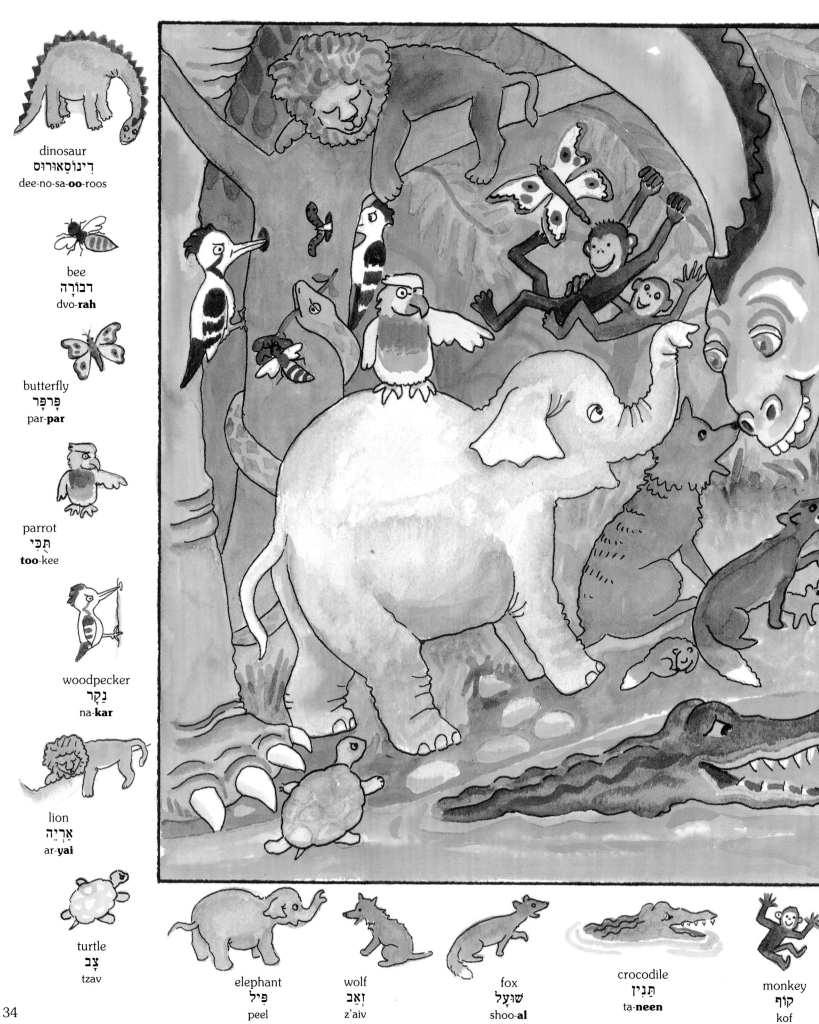

monkey
קוֹף
kof

camel
גָּמָל
ga-**mal**

deer
צְבִי
tz'vee

zebra
זֶבְּרָה
ze-brah

giraffe
ג׳ירָפָה
jee-**ra**-fah

tiger
נָמֵר
na-**mair**

fly
זְבוּב
zvoov

porcupine
דָּרְבָּן
dar-**ban**

worm
תּוֹלַעַת
to-**la**-at

peacock
טַוָּס
ta-**vas**

kangaroo
קֶנְגוּרוּ
ken-goo-**roo**

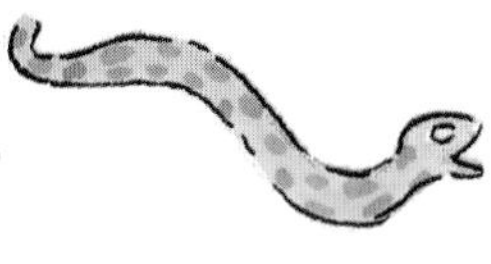

snake
נָחָשׁ
na-**ḥash**

hippopotamus
בְּהֵמוֹת
bi-hai-**mot**

rabbit
שָׁפָן
sha-**fan**

Work and Play

עֲבוֹדָה וָנֹפֶשׁ a-vo-**dah** va-**no**-fesh

Dictionary מִלּוֹן mee-**lon**

A
Ahashveros, 19
animals, 34
apartment, 10
aqueduct, 28
Arab, 29
ark, 12
ark curtain, 12
astronaut, 36
aunt, 5
autumn, 22

B
baby, 5
baby boy, 25
baby girl, 25
bar/bat mitzvah, 25
barn, 30
basketball, 11
bathtub, 4
Be seeing you, 8
bed, 4
bee, 34
bells, 13
bicycle, 11
birthday, 24
birthday cake, 25
bitter herb, 13
Bless you, 8
bone, 13
bookbag, 14
books, 14
booth (sukkah), 17
boots, 6
boy, 19
braids, 7
bread, 33
breastplate, 13
bridal canopy, 24
bride, 24
bridge, 30
broom, 4
brother, 5
bulletin board, 14
bus, 11
bush, 31
butter, 33
butterfly, 34

C
cactus, 29
calendar, 7
camel, 35
campfire, 20
candelabra, 12
candles, 16
cantor, 12
car, 11
carpenter, 36
cat, 4
cemetery, 26
chair, 15
charity, 27
cheese, 32
chicken, 30
chicken (food), 32
children, 20
chimney, 17
church, 29
circle dance (hora), 31
circumcision, 25
circumciser (mohel), 25
citron, 17
city, 28
clarinet, 24
class, 15
climbing bars, 15
clock, 6
clouds, 20
clown, 36
commandment, 27
computer, 5
confirmation, 25
Congratulations, 8
cookies, 33
country, 30
cousin, 5
cow, 30
crocodile, 34
crown, 13
cup, 33

D
dairy, 32
dancer, 36
dancing school, 10
daughter, 7
deer, 35
dinosaur, 34
dish, 32
doctor, 36
dog, 4
dreidel, 18
dress, 6
driver, 36

E
ear, 7
earrings, 14
egg, 13
eggs, 33
eight, 23
elephant, 18,34
Elijah's chair, 25
Esther, 19
eternal light, 12
etrog box, 13
Excuse me, 8
eye, 7
eyeglasses, 14

F
factory, 28
family, 5
farmers, 30
father, 5
felafel sandwich, 28
fence, 31
fighter plane, 29
fireplace, 5
fish, 31
fisherman, 31
five, 23
flag, 18
flour, 33
flowers, 25
fly, 35
food, 24
foot, 7
fork, 33
four, 23
fox, 34
Friday, 21
friends, 24
fruit, 17, 32
fruit and nuts mixture, 6
funeral, 26

G
game, 7
garbage, 33
gardener, 36
gifts, 25
giraffe, 35
girl, 19
glass, 33
globe, 14
goat, 19
God, 23
godfather, 25
good deeds, 27
Good morning, 8
Good night, 9
Good week, 16
Good-bye, 8

grandfather, 5
grandmother, 5
greens, 13
grocery store, 10
groom, 24
guests, 17, 25
guitar, 6

H
haggadah, 18
hair, 7
hallah, 16
Haman, 19
hand, 7
Hanukkah, 19
Hanukkah lamp, 18
Happy birthday, 9
Happy Hanukkah, 16
Happy holiday, 16
happy times, 24
hat, 6
havdalah candle, 13
Have a good trip, 8
head, 7
Hearty appetite, 9
helicopter, 29
Hello, 8
Help! 8
hike, 30
hippopotamus, 35
holiday greetings, 16
holidays, 18
Holocaust Remembrance Day, 26
Holy Temple, 26
honey, 17
horse, 30
house, 4
How do you say...?, 9

I
I love you, 9
ice cream, 33
in the country, 30
in the kitchen, 33
in-laws, 24
Israel Independence Day, 20

J
jacket, 6
jam, 33
Jeep, 10

K
kangaroo, 35
kibbutz, 28
kindness to animals, 27
king, 19
kitchen, 32
knee, 7
knife, 33

L
Lag Ba'Omer, 20
lake, 31
lion, 34
lulav (branches of willow, myrtle, and palm), 17

M
Maccabees, 18
mailman, 10
map, 14
market, 29
May you be written and sealed for a good year, 16
May you be written down for a good year, 16
meat, 32
memorial lamp, 26
mezuzah, 13
milk, 33
Monday, 21
monkey, 34
monkey bars, 15
Mordecai, 19
Moses, 20
mosque, 28
mother, 5
motorcycle, 11
Mount Sinai, 20
mourner, 26
mouth, 7
movie house, 11
musicians, 24

N
naming ceremony, 25
neighborhood, 10
New Year's cards, 17
night, 20
nine, 23
Ninth of Av, 26
No, 9
noisemaker, 19
nose, 7
notebook, 15
numbers, 23

O
Oh, no, 9
olive tree, 29
one, 23
orange tree, 29

P
pajamas, 6
palm tree 29
parachutist, 36
parade, 20
parliament of Israel, 28
parrot, 34
parve, 32
passenger plane, 29
Passover, 19
Passover seder dish, 13
Passover seder, 19
peace, 8
Peaceful and blessed Sabbath, 16
peacock, 35
pen, 15
pencil, 14
People of Israel, 20
phylacteries (tefillin), 13
play (recreation), 36
playground, 14
Please, 9
policewoman, 11
porcupine, 35
post office, 11
pot, 32
prayer book, 12
prayer book for High Holidays, 12
prayer shawl, 12
principal, 14
Purim, 19
Purim pastries, 19
Purim scroll, 13

Q
queen, 19

R
rabbi, 12
rabbit, 35
radio, 7
ram's horn, 13
reading from prophets, 25
reading platform, 12
refrigerator, 32
responsibility for each other, 27
ritual objects, 13
river, 30
Rosh Hashanah (New Year), 17

S
Sabbath, 16
Sabbath bread (hallah), 16
salt, 33
Saturday, 21
school, 14
scissors, 15
scribe, 36
sea, 29
seasons, 22
seder book (haggadah), 18
seven days of mourning, 26
seven, 23
Shavuot, 21
shirt, 6
Shivah, 26
shoes, 20
shopping cart, 10
shorts, 6
shower, 7
sidewalk, 20
Simhat Torah, 18
singer, 36
singing group, 31
sink, 4
sister, 5
six, 23
skirt, 6
skunk, 31
slide, 5
snake, 35
snorkel, 28
soap, 6
soccer player, 36
socks, 6
soldier, 18, 19
son, 7
soup, 32
spice box, 13
spoon, 33
spring, 22
squirrel, 17
stairs, 4
star, 17
State of Israel, 28
stool, 7
store, 10
stove, 32
stroller, 10
student, 14
sugar, 33
Sukkot, 17
summer, 22
summer camp, 30
sun, 20
Sunday, 21
Sweet dreams, 9
swing, 15
sword, 18
synagogue, 12

T
table, 4
tailor, 36
tank, 28
teacher, 14
teeth, 7
television, 4
temple, 12
Ten Commandments, 20
ten, 23
tennis player, 36
tent, 31
Thanks, 9
thief, 36
three, 23
Thursday, 21
tiger, 35
toilet, 4
tombstone, 26
toothbrush, 7
top (dreidel), 18
Torah, 13
Torah mantle, 13
Torah parade, 18
Torah pointer, 13
Torah study, 27
tourists, 28
toys, 10
tractor, 30
traffic light, 10
train, 30
tree, 19
truck, 11
Tu Bi-Sh'vat, 19
Tuesday, 21
turtle, 34
two, 23

U
ultra-Orthodox Jew, 29
uncle, 5

V
vegetables, 32
village, 28
violin, 24
visiting the sick, 27

W
water, 33
wave, 29
Wear it well, 9
wedding, 24
Wednesday, 21
week, 21
Western Wall, 29
window, 7
Windsurfer, 28
wine, 16
winter, 22
wolf, 34
woodpecker, 34
woods, 31
work, 36
worm, 35
Wow, super, 9

Y
Yes, 9
Yom Kippur (Day of Atonement), 17

Z
zebra, 35

About the Author

Chaya M. Burstein and her husband, Mordy, have built a house on a mountain top in northern Israel. Chaya fits in the work of writing and illustrating books among painting, plastering, and digging in the garden.

For many years before moving to Israel, Chaya lived in Hicksville, Long Island, New York, where she raised three children and one cat. She has written and illustrated fifteen books for children including *The Jewish Kids Catalog*, published by The Jewish Publication Society, and *Rivka Grows Up*. Both of these books won the National Jewish Book Award. Chaya's second book for JPS, *A Kid's Catalog of Israel*, was named a Notable Children's Trade Book in the Field of Social Studies.